GLADE OF LIGHT

By

MARIA DULCE LEITAO REIS

DEDICATION

I deeply thank God Almighty Father and all the people who have been and are part of my path.

EDITOR'S REVIEW

Written in the state of witty and intelligent thoughts, Maria Dulce Leitão Reis returns to bring to us *Glade of Light:* a book that is done with great excellence, showing her continual battle against the painful realities of life. This book is a living proof that the author has continued walking on her path seeking for a light: a light for which many of us are also seeking: a light that would somehow illuminate the path we are walking on and give courage to our ongoing battle against the intricacies of life.

This book certainly tells us that we are not alone in dealing with our pains, hardships, incompleteness or sacrifices. Maria Dulce Leitão Reis has so engraved in this book the brilliant words of poetry and rhymed truths that come from her innermost self, mind and soul. While she has continued to fight injustices and the harrowing betrayal of someone from the past, she, however, never stops appreciating the beauty and wonders of love, family, nature, forgiveness and resilience, as well as her deep innate spiritual relation to the Almighty God.

I am very thankful that Maria Dulce Leitão Reis has chosen me to proofread, edit and review at least 4 of her excellent books, among others, that make up such great contributions to the world of adept poets and brilliant poetry. Maria Dulce Leitão Reis is, without doubt, one of those proficient and creative genius poets in the world today, who have never relinquished their ardent affection towards meaningful poetry. To be her editor, moreover, is quite a prestige and honour because it gives me an opportunity for advancement and teaches my very own self to stay strong despite enormous and colossal challenges of life.

The never-ending uncertainties and vicissitudes that we are experiencing in life help us understand that we live in a natural world. And not in a fairy-tale zone which we are told to believe in a magical, imaginary perfect world, free from sadness or sorrow. We are, of course, subject to bouts of pains and obstacles, losses and failures. And *Glade of Light* teaches us to embrace those realities. This book is precisely a must-read as it inspires us to move forward with life.

Junfil Olarte, Editor
Calamba, Laguna, 12 September 2020

Editor's short biography:

Junfil Olarte is a freelance editor for poetry books and novels working with several authors from different countries in the world. A travel writer, author and musician who started documenting his journeys in early 2004, Junfil Olarte originally held a degree in the aviation industry prior to becoming a writer and has already written and edited many articles, novels and poetry books. He lives in the Philippine Islands.

REVIEW:

Glade of Light by Maria Dulce Leitão Reis

This poetic note intends to highlight some psychological features of the author, as well as some aspects of her already appreciable work.

Between the latter and the first book published *Nascer do Sol* in 2018, it has 14 more titles, of which 8 are translated into English. There are 56 collective participations (the first in 2012) in Portuguese and foreign collections - some in English -. There is an improvement in his poetic record, in my view, commendable. It is always a delight to read her writings as when she allows us to analyze them informally and when she edits them.

A lady with a strong personality, optimistic by nature and creative, she gives her work an inner strength that leads us to experience each verse, savouring as she says at a certain point … *with the strength restored, I set the table and savour my dinner, because I deserve it…* and she does, even if she's alone.

And she dreams, in the transcendence and in the search for her Self, she dreams and loves an awkward *wolf mother.*

Body and spirit, she breathes poetry. She sings, deliciously, as if she writes notes on a sheet of paper and turns them into pieces of love.

In this book Glade of Light, she seeks to get out of the forest in which she has entered and reach the glade in her life because every day is a day of deserved light.

May you find, my friend, that light that relieves you of the cross of the path you have chosen and keeps your smile as a reward - for the pains you have suffered - even if the roof falls on you.

Very successful.

Porto, 7 July 2020
Maria Beatriz Ferreira

Brief biographical note:

Maria Beatriz Ferreira is from Porto district (1950), married and resident in Maia city.
She has a degree in History from the Faculty of Letters of the University of Porto (1983) and a Master in Public Administration from the University of Minho (1998).
She has dedicated herself to writing since 1976, photography and painting at a later stage in her life.

PREFACE

Glade of Light is another book by the poet and writer Maria Dulce Leitão Reis. In it, the author quenches the thirst of our being with its sublimated inspiration in the poems, where she cultivates the veracity and grandeur of her essence. She draws – with simple letters – silences, cries, longings, projects and harmonious hymns, full of feelings and praises, letting the poems become paintings on the paper canvas of her sensations and affections.

The author cultivates in her spirit an exalted sensitivity by the search for an intangible made palpable.

You can read in an excerpt from her extraordinary poem Song of Love: *I follow the notes / of the melody / convinced / that they will / take me / to the place / where I belong / I will go in search of me.* In this and other poems, we found an immeasurable susceptibility because this great lady became a prodigy of contemporary Portuguese poetry, overflowing her gift, her genius to praise with mastery, her ethical values, and the greatness of the magic message in a relevant and dignified way, as she elevates phrases to a Higher World.

In this book of poetry, nothing is superficial. The author works with great autonomy, the philosophical, mystical verses and those that come out of the heart, populating the universe of her knowledge, with more stars in a strong emotionality, as if time framed the clear space of her way of being and be in life.

Maria Dulce Leitão Reis possesses an emotive and strong symbol, capable of putting light even on those who, at first sight, do not understand the immensity of her serious and authentic writing, coloured with the pollen of the most beautiful and exotic flowers, that inhabit at her core.

Her poems are tied with rare and immensely gratifying ties due to their form and content in the germination of the extraordinary seed of shared wisdom of affective fullness, where we adhere and share the knowledge of the linked texts, in power and in touch, which allows the dictated balance, written in the beautiful poetic satins as worn by the author on the nights of the days full of revelations and experiences, but illuminated by invincible dawns.

The value of this work, of this book, is in its existential potential, where the past, the present and the voice of a future are spoken, which does not generate individualism but gratitude and donation.

The poet and writer Maria Dulce Leitão Reis is unique in the way of writing sensations without wasting time with ambiguities.

She is a woman of strong and intelligent nature, seductive, of great inner and outer beauty, with no time for insignificant things. She does not measure distances when she has in mind a trail that takes her to a better world. She cultivates the gift of friendship in a joy expressed in the landscape of her being.

Glade of Light is the book where the diamond is sculpted for the greatness of the chosen words from which the most beautiful poems are extracted, which dignify those who made them.

It leaves a taste in the senses of the most attentive reader because the themes flow from the depths of a great soul. They please and thrill due to the greatness and sensitivity of their author.

Gloria Marreiros
Portimão, July 2020

TABLE OF CONTENTS

GLADE OF LIGHT

I opened the door and left
A breath of fresh air
Said good morning to me
I replied with a smile
It was all I needed
To convince me
That I would have
A wonderful day!

I entered the forest
Towards the glade of light.

A flock of birds
Kept me company
They were woodpeckers, crows
Some more fearless seagulls
(The sea was falling behind)
Goldfinches, nightingales, larks
Macaws, parrots, sparrows
And there was a bluebird
Some sang nice
But they were all good company
And I sang a song with them
Those who didn't know how to sing
They did pirouettes
It was their way of dancing!

We reached the glade of light
We relieved ourselves of the Cross.

We sat on the floor
In crossed legs
We held hands
We sang a hymn praising life
We were from all nations
And all different
But all brothers
We had something in common
Plenty of love in our hearts!

Uplifting and inspiring path
Walk made with joy!

SONG OF LOVE

I follow
The notes
Of the melody
Convinced
That will lead me
To the place
Where
I belong

I will go in search of me...

I stayed
Somewhere
Forgotten
In the time!
Half hibernated
Half awake.
I woke up
To the sound
Of the melody
Of my song
Of love!

THE WHISPER OF THE WIND

...And the wind passed
And whispered meekly in my ear
I love you!
The words of the wind
Gave me the courage
And cheered me up
Softened my heart
Enchanted my soul
Lifted my body, dolent and weak.
It was the fuel
That fueled my being!

Love
It's a powerful magic potion.

Only love makes one growing!

BECAUSE I DESERVE

I get home
Hungry and tired
More dead than alive
The hustle and bustle of everyday life
But now
I am in my sacred stronghold
And I deserve the best.

I get rid of my clothes
That cover my body
I give it back its freedom
I stretch out on the chaise longue
I feel tiredness
Escaping freely
Through my pores
A wave of well-being
Envelops me
In a seductive ambience
I drink greedily
Savour slow
All the remission that covers me
Because I deserve.

With forces regained
I get up and go to take a shower
To give me my holy finish!

I make my dinner.

I set the table
Linen and lace white tablecloth
And my best tableware
I light the candles and incenses
I play a soft music
Because I Deserve
I dine alone with me
And I enjoy my delicious meal
Because I deserve!

Epilogue:

Because I got home extremely tired, I could have just eaten a sandwich sitting on the couch in front of the telly. After all, it was just me. This procedure would put me at a disadvantage before me, because before me, I deserve the best. Instead, I tried to give myself a great treatment. I relaxed on the chaise longue, took a bath with bath salts and white rose petals. I hydrated my body with a good moisturizer. I had a good dinner and serenely enjoyed all the treats I had toast myself.
Won the body and won the spirit. I was happy, because I deserve.
We are the ones who sew our happiness.

I GOT THE BEST OF THEE

For me
It was accomplished
But I didn't stay with you.

Yet...
I got the best of thee.

Your loving gaze
Your soft caress
As soft as velvet
Your warm smile
Your essence
Involving me like a chenille blanket
Of tranquility and coziness
As soft as velvet!

I didn't stay with you
But you left me the most
Everything!

Your gaze
Your smile
Your caress
Your essence

Lavish seeds...

And when the last day comes
We will meet in the azure
And we will belong to each other
Forever!

MY POETRY IS YOU

My poetry is you
I read this phrase somewhere
It stuck in my mind
And in my heart.

My poetry is you...

I spell each word slowly
And allow me to be possessed
By the magic and magnetism
Of each word
When I finish the sentence
I am in ecstasy
And you are in front of me
I don't know if I breathe
If I float
If I'm awake
Or if I'm dreaming.
I'm delighted!
Your image, your energy
Completely fills me.

My poetry is you...

You are the sap
That dews me every morning
You are the colours of the sunset

That make me drunk with seduction
You are the moonlight
That possesses me with love
And takes me to cloud nine
Making me scream
With pleasure and freedom.

Honey, you are my king
You are my poetry
You are my everything!

OWNED BY DESIRE

The boat of life already shows somewhere
It's been quite an adventure!

On the crest of the waves
I faced the fury of the sea
In meekness, I beheld the stars
And I fell asleep snuggled
By the moonlight that dripped from the moon
On the beach sand, I built castles
So as not to lose the way of playing.

I settled in hope
Owned by desire
To find my love.

I prepared a delicious cocktail
With a good dash of dream
I put Aida de Verdi on the CD player
And leaned back on the chaise-long
Letting me being possessed
By the beauty of the symphony
While being captivated
By the mixture of the amazing flavours
Of my delicious beet cocktail.

I travelled through places
Never dreamed of before

Virgin nooks
Altars in prayer
Of perfumed love and hope
The sweetness of looks
Reassured the heart
That blossomed into a beautiful flower.

I settled in hope
Owned by desire
To find my love!

WASTED TIME

I keep saying
The designs of God
Are unfathomable
There are things not worth
Try to understand
Nor look for answers
Because I never get them
There are things that go beyond
My earthly understanding.

I learned to adapt
To things less good
Without making it a drama
I wrap them in tissue paper
I tie them with satin bows
And keep them in the tabernacle
From my heart
Where there is only love
And I convince myself
Are special gifts.

I learned to shape myself
To the situations
Lest they cause me friction
And don't hurt me.
I learned to build
The way I live

With me and others
I called it happiness.
What is happiness?

Happiness is not a slogan
It's not a stipulated thing
It's something that each one builds
To your own measure
So that you feel good
Everyday
I build mine
Everyday I try to add
Another parallel to my path.

Those who spend their lives moaning
Don't have time to build anything
Waste valuable time
That could have used to be happy!

ARID LAND

Life is screwed
Things are done with love
And we get a kick!

It's confusing
Seeing human being
Didn't learn to sow love ...

A truth that I know so well.

On arid land
Selfishness is king!

MY LITTLE THINGS

These are the little things
That make me love life
And that's how I'm happy!

Growing a potato
A tomato, a bean, a cabbage
Prune a rose bush
Planting pansies
Petunias, geraniums
Cacti and succulents...
And writing my blabbering!

I love to see my plants grow
Blooming and bear fruit.
I like to have breakfast
Walking around the garden
While saying good morning
To its tenants
I caught this addiction
A long time ago
And that's how the morning meal
Tastes so good and special to me
Here I continue to do the same
I see no need to change
This old custom of mine
That gives me
So much pleasure and satisfaction!

Inspiration for my writings...
I also have problems
Aches and pains
Like any ordinary mortal
However
I don't let myself be overwhelmed by them
I react and fight
I don't let them stop me
From savouring my little pleasures
Conductor channels of energy
And good mood
That help me help others
And to me too!

These are the little things
That make me love life
And that's how I'm happy!

I'M THE DAUGHTER OF THE WIND AND SEA BREEZE

I'm the daughter of the wind and sea breeze
I'm granddaughter of Mother Nature
From father wind, I inherited the genius
Docile on the day of the heatwave
Furious on a stormy day
I inherited the sea, from mother breeze
In the valley of the waves
I write my verses
Each letter is a star
Each word is a constellation
Giving light and path
To those who, like me,
Wander around the universe
In search of love and affection
Grandma mother nature, left me the vastness
Where I stretch and snuggle
Under the leafy trees
And I take a nap
Intoxicated by the scent of wildflowers.

I run free through the fresh
Clean, sunny fields
With open arms thanking the Lord
I stuff myself with wild blackberries
Sorrel, rockrose flowers

And I get down on my knees praising God
For the delicious food.

I am the daughter of freedom
I'm the daughter of the wind and sea breeze!

No need to go all over the place
Happiness is ahead of us
In the small and common things
It only takes humility, tactfulness
And some wisdom
At the top of the varied beaker that our life is
A good dose of gratitude
Closes our crossing with a flourish!

I'm the daughter of the wind and sea breeze.
I'm a friend of sorrow and joy!

TREASURE

There was no light...
But anyway
I entered the darkroom
The scent that floated there
Intoxicated my nostrils
Lit up my mind
Warmed my heart!

You had been there
But I didn't make it in time...

I don't regret
Of having entered the darkroom
I got your smell
Ingrained in my skin!

I AM NOT A ROBOT

I'm not a robot
I'm a human being
Made of butter
Melting
With a tear
A smile
A gaze
A kiss
A hug
A handshake
A flower caught in the bush
A thorn stuck in the skin
To pick a blackberry up
From the brambles!

I'm not a robot
I'm a human being
Made of butter
Hardening
With the lie
Selfishness
Inhumanity
Greed
The slouch
Arrogance
The lack of humility
Neglect

The revenge
The hate
The trampling of human rights.

We also have
A program
Inserted within us
A program
That God did for us
With love and for love
So let's stick to it
Because that's the will
And the gift of God
It's the safe conduct
For a full life!

A vehement yes, to love.

CLOUD NINE

... And the wind was my friend
My companion and my lover
He kissed my tears
Framed my smile
And made love to me
It took me through unknown
And absolutely stunning corners
It also took me
To the most degraded places on the planet
So that I was absolutely aware of reality
Life is not just good things
There are also a lot of bad things
It is important to be informed and aware
In order to find
The best way to contribute
We can all help
Improving the place where we live
Be it on a social level
Or on an environmental level
If each one of us plants a flower
We will make the world a beautiful garden
Looking only at our navel
Is pure narcissism
Who guarantees us
That there are no navels
More beautiful than ours?

You need to open your eyes wide
And look at a 360° radius
By helping others, we help ourselves
The world is a gear
Each of us is a tooth of the cog
And we contribute to the cog to work well
More dividends, more joy
More health, more comfort
More beauty, more well-being
More peace, more happiness.

We are all here to be happy
That's what everyone says
Each one wants their Nirvana
To attain a state of bliss
And we all know it's true
We all deserve to feel blessed
We all deserve to be on top of the world
Shall we battle for our cloud nine?
Guys come on!

AFTER DUSK A REDEMPTIVE DAWN

Twilight falls on me
Laden with fog and heavy smoke.
Fear and the spectre of death
Prowl my senses
I feel myself like clothes twisting
Inside the washing machine
I try to escape from myself
And I don't see the way out
My head almost bursting
I blacked out.

I honestly thought
I was dead
I remember the affliction
Of wanting to escape
And when I reached the peak
A sense of peace and freedom
Enveloped me
In fear, I opened my eyes
And pinched myself
But the doubt remained
Did I die or am I still alive?

I feel light and calm
Wrapped in transparency
And tied with incenses
I rock myself

Pushed by the pleasant feeling
Of detachment
Miracles happen
What was black before
It is now colorful and shiny
I spread my sight
Rotating in all directions
I have no parietal eye
I'm not a chameleon
But I feel me the eye of a giant flower.

We can live better
If we don't board
On the pessimistic vessel of pain
We can live better
If we paint the world in another colour
The colours of happiness
Red, white, pink or orange
The sky is already blue
And the colour of the sun is yellow
Most of the work is already done
God took care of this task!

The dusk has faded
Taking all the pain
Making room
To a redemptive dawn
Dewed with gratitude and love!

MY ROOTS- Here and there

I am here
In this place for so long
Here I took roots
An upright trunk
Glossy foliage and verdant
And in summer, I fill myself
With blue and white flowers.

I won't see my flowers anymore
Specials, exotics
Scented with hopes.

I won't be here anymore
To see my hydrangea bloom
My sweet peas and pansies
Camellias, daffodils, hollyhocks
And so many more...
I won't be here anymore
to see my roses flourish
I won't be here anymore
To do the pruning
I won't be here anymore
to see my trees grow
Another year and the peach tree
Will bear fruit
I won't be here anymore
To eat the sweet figs

Of the fig tree I planted
I won't be here anymore
To scare away the blackbirds
Not to eat my figs
But they had enough...
I will no longer see people
Who passed by me
Nor those I greeted!

Tears flow with emotion...

I learned to love
The simple things in my life
It will not be easy
Pluck my roots from this ground
I will pull myself carefully
So as not to damage my roots
I will have to replant me
In the other place, where I am going!

RETURN TO THE BEGINNING

There are still beautiful gestures
Imbued with romanticism and kindness
There are still those
Who offer a red rose!

You were my first love ...
It was a great passion
But ...
There was a mismatch
That changed our lives
It was written so
On the paths of heaven
The Creator's designs are unfathomable.

I think we read the wrong book
Or so...
We couldn't read the signs
Were they hieroglyphics?

The truth is that life
Mine and yours
Went around and around
Although we didn't match
We always walked on parallel paths
So parallel
That even though I didn't know
Where you were

I felt your presence
A similar relationship
To the relationship between the two eyes
As someone said
They blink together
Move together
Cry together
See things together
Sleep together
And they never see each other
That's how true friendship should be!

Donation
Complicity
Detachment from futility
Expect nothing in return
From part to part
No favour ...

All good feelings
Are built on the stone of friendship
Are plastered with kindness
And painted with love!
That even though I didn't know
Where you were.

THE IDIOT BITES HIS OWN TAIL

I empty my mind
Because I don't want to think about anything
The ostrich
Also hides its head in the sand
Thinking that the danger passes
And does not see it
What is this?
Naivety?
Ignorance?
The solution is not!

Ignoring does not solve anything
It is a certificate of stupidity
That we pass on to ourselves
It is very sad and discouraging
Rewarding ourselves
With such a certificate
Per us and for us
We must always do and want
Honourable praises
The affronts
That others unjustly make us
Are enough!

Evil does not pay
It is not justified
It does not serve anyone well

And ends up returning
To those who did it.
That others consider us stupid
It doesn't matter
If we are well-resolved people
It will not give us the slightest dent
Because we are aware
Of our values
And as such
We know how to use them
In our favour
And in favour of others
In doing so
We are worthy
Of the place we occupy in life
In society and on the planet!

I take this opportunity
To mention some popular sayings
That illustrate what I just said.

A dog that barks, does not bite.
Dogs bark and the caravan passes.
By carriage's pace you can see who's inside.
Donkey voices don't reach heaven.
Finally, a saying
That I just made up myself.

The idiot bites his own tail!

GOOD FOOTPRINTS

Don't be shy to say I love you
Do not inhibit yourself to love
Do not be shy
To bare your heart
It feels so good knowing
That someone loves us
It's good to feel
But also important to hear
You have to listen
-I love you
I can't live without you
You are the water that refreshes me
The wine that makes me drunk
In an aphrodisiac welfare!

It's like the decoration
Of a delicious cake
Before tasting the cake
It's the decoration
That causes the first impact
An initial sensation
Only then comes the flavour!
Cake decoration
It resembles foreplay
That precedes any successful task!

Life is so short

If we don't pay attention
To what really matters
We have reached the last day
And we realize
That we haven't done the essentials
Because we forgot to love
Our time is precious
Let us take advantage of it
To love those who love us
To love those around us
One day
When someone who loves us
Passes away, in our presence
We will regret
The time we wasted
Wasted time is empty time
Time devoid of love
There is nothing more rewarding
That giving and receiving love
We only receive what we give
We only reap what we sow
If I plant potatoes
I can't harvest beets!

Our value and our satisfaction
Is not in the goods we have accumulated
On passing away
We leave everything
Things that time will reduce to dust
But if we love those who love us
We will stay alive forever

In our hearts
We will leave serenely
No guilt and no remorse
With a light soul, stripped of spite
Having left full of giving and receiving
Having kissed and hugged often
We leave love, we take love
We accomplished our mission.

We leave good footprints
That others will follow!

ALWAYS

If I were a she wolf
And had found
A helpless baby
I would breastfeed him
It is written naturally
In my heart.

My family
It has always been my priority
I always forgot about me
My needs
Became secondary
Yet I don't care
Because I think I can handle
With my pains
What matters to me
Is being able to relieve pain
And supply the needs
The ones I love.

Never anyone
Hear me moaning
Or curse my luck
Regret a decision
Because I understand that life
Is a blessing
Being a caregiver

Is a grace and a gift
That God has reserved
Fully in my heart
It's so surprising
Comforting
And rewarding
Feel that those in my care
Breath my affection
Became addicted to my fondness
Forgetting for a moment
Their sorrow, their pain ...

My heart
Will always be a nest
Warm and cute
Where there will always be love!

EMPATHY AND COMPASSION

I'm very clumsy
To deal with ambiguity
I don't know if I like meat or fish
Cold or hot
Whether I go or stay
What the hell
We need to be resourceful and determined
Otherwise, we are not going anywhere
Doubt, indecision
It won't let us take a step
Beware of ambiguous people
We never know what to say or do
We never know
What mask they are wearing
Because of the disparity in its characteristics
Definitely
They are not trusted people!

Feelings of pain
Anger and accommodation
They lodge in my heart
I'm clumsy
To deal with superficial people
With limited horizons
I like who spreads themselves
In endless horizons
People who hug, kiss, laugh

And jump for no reason
People who scream the truth
Without fear of tearing the infinite
I don't like cynical people
Hypocritical and ambiguous people
Deep down, I feel sorry
For these bad and mean people.

I feel compassion and empathy
For other's unhappiness
Through compassion
We try to relieve someone else's suffering
Compassion
Suggests unjustly inflicted suffering
Because if it's fair
There is no need to have compassion
Having compassion is a sign
That we still have humanitarian emotions
Although inhumanity
Strides forward
To have compassion is to be altruistic
It's forgetting about us
To help others
There are already a few
Those who suffer the pain of others
As if they were theirs
Humanity
It lacks empathy and compassion
It walks over the edge
And probably extinction
Coldness, wickedness

With which we perpetuate acts of torture
Inhumanity
Self-centeredness
They take us that way.

Empathy and compassion
Two crucial ingredients
In building peace
Empathy and compassion
Two essential ingredients
In its maintenance!

BLACK TOURMALINE

A long long time ago
I left on a trip
A circumnavigation
Around myself
The goal was to reach my core
I faced several obstacles
There were storms
There were typhoons
As well as icebergs
I faced anacondas and sharks
Yet
The most painful obstacles
Were the misunderstanding
Ill will
Intolerance
Inhumanity
Of the people who crossed my path
Helpful to me
Was courage
Fearlessness
Discernment
Even complacency.

The hardness of battles
Made me more agile and stronger
Today nothing downs me
I was luckier

Then Fernao de Magalhães
I returned to my roots
I completed my adventure
I reached my core
Today I like to sit down
In the balustrade of my life
Looking without haste
With eyes teary with tenderness
My indigo sky
Where I see
My most secret longings
Impregnated with mysticism and magic
Without clouds embargoing my sun
That warms, seduces and energizes me
Moved by this cozy solar wave
I caress my black tourmaline
That I keep with devotion
It also protects me and drives me away
Of the negative energies.

I won this stone
In one of my wanderings
When patiently
I was trying to reach my core
My private island
Where I feast
With rare and exotic fruits
It was here that God offered me
The black tourmaline
He knew
That I would need this wonder

To take to good port
My daring adventure
And it went like this
That I managed to get back to my roots
Today I sit quietly
In the balustrade of my life
Looking without haste
With eyes teary with tenderness
My indigo sky
Where I drink serenity and love
Holding in my hand
My black tourmaline!

DARKNESS AND CLARITY

I go by the hand of darkness
She promised to take me to the light
Without further ado, I trusted her blindly
The road is inhospitable and very long
I start to get apprehensive and anxious
I'm getting to be afraid
Fear sets in
Finally, I am overcome with panic
I scream wildly
But no one comes to my aid
The darkness is on spider palps
To control me
My despair is too great
Because I feel cheated by her
How did I get fooled?
This thought
It becomes my own torture
I get stuck in the maze
Where despair led me
I look stunned in all directions
And I don't see the way out
The darkness tries to calm me down
But without success
I already labelled it
As an enemy to slaughter.

Unexpectedly, but only for me

Because of despair
My judgment was dulled
A point of light
Begins to form at a distance
A glimpse of hope
Loomed in my eyes
And a slight smile
In the left corner of my mouth
My wish is to start running
I am thirsty and hungry for clarity
Darkness
Although it's no longer as severe
Brakes my will
Prevents compulsion.

In a streak of intelligence
And common sense
I decide to be calm and patient
When walking slowly, without haste
I have time to observe
Increasing the light point
That will quench my discomfort
I have time to absorb the approach
From the air perfumed
By the scent of flowers
To hear the birds chirping
I have time
To give my brain time
To record, assimilate
And archive everything in proper order
In order to give me order
To enter the light
Completely free!

THE RETURN

I returned
From my travels around the world
I stayed long hours
Admiring the wheat field
Spotted poppies
The hayfield
Rippling in the wind
Bringing to me
The sweet and warm smell
The towering oak
Strong and leafy
Housing all the birds
Seeking protection
In his safe branches
It made me remember my father
My lighthouse and my shelter
The sun was warm and bright
It reminded me of my mother's lap
Cozy, warm!

I sat down with my parents
In the twilight of their lives
I looked deeply into their eyes
I saw myself in them and I felt blessed
Now I was sure
That my place was here
Divine Providence

Put father and mother
In my care.

God blessed me
With the greatest grace
That life could give me
Being able to take care
Who took care of me
I feel like I can reward them
By my absence
For the kisses and hugs, I didn't give them
I feel rewarded
Through years of suffering and struggle
For the chance to be able to pamper them now
My greatest gift to them
It's my availability
My love and affection
To make them feel loved
Dear ones, needed
To make them feel that they still matter!

I know that age brings mumbling
Impatience and other annoyances
Undoubtedly an attractive challenge
Which is easy ...
It doesn't take us any further.

When I think of the abandoned elderly
Amongst people who ignore and neglect them
Even their own kith and kin
My eyes are watery

An elusive tear
Roll over my cheek
And fall into the crystal bowl
The care cup!

Take care...
It is not to do in two strokes
In a hurry to go somewhere
Take care...
Is not in a hurry
Everything else can wait
Is to be attentive to the slightest blink
The most imperceptible gasp
Oh river of life
Let me navigate you
But don't make too many waves
That my vessel is delicate
Take me back
To the sea of affections
Where all things live
That mom and dad
They taught me to know!

Now it's me who prepares
The chamomile tea and a cookie
Now it's me singing for them
The lullaby
For a beautiful fall asleep
And a night of restful sleep
I will sing every day
The song I made up

Dad and mum
My time is yours
Use it for your total pleasure
I am here
To teach you how to live
Positively
With joy
Very calmly
With much peace
With love.

I was extremely moved
See that in 67 years of union
There are still declarations of love!
I'm a lucky one
For watching
A rare and beautiful moment
That moment will be engraved in gold
In my soul and in my heart
Grateful to life and to God for generosity
I grew up with bad things
I was rewarded with good things
The gifts You placed in my saddlebag
Your blessing, my Lord.

A DREAM PLACE

Burning in desire
I contemplate the moon
I dream that I live in a lunar castle
And I look forward to see
My big and so loved love!

I can already hear his steps
In the diamond sand
Are music notes to my ears
The most exquisite symphony!

The simple flower he offered me
Touched my heart deeply...

I pray to Almighty God
To keep forever by my side
This precious love
And hope
In a diaphanous universe
Make our planet
A dream place
Where we can all live
In enchantment and pleasure!

NOW YES

This exasperating pain
Started in the heel
It looks like revenge
So I can't walk
I had so many dreams
I had made so many plans
But I'm not
To let me be quiet
abandoned to luck
That the wicked witch cursed me
I will continue to chase
My dreams
And one by one
I will make them come true.

First of all
I'll need to untangle myself
Of the webs that bind me
Of the dust that suffocates me
From the darkness that scares me
I relax
And I try to reason clearly
I know it won't be easy
Find the solution
For this piece of work
But it's not impossible
Step by step

Faltering in the beginning
But more and more firmly
I do not give up
In the midst of all this misfortune
I will find a glade
The darkness is not so dense anymore
I can already hear in the distance
The birds chirping
And calling for me
A beautiful waterfall!

It was a heavenly vision
Fresh and crystal clear water
Coming from the heights
Falling into a turquoise pool
Where little fish swarm
Of all colours and shapes
Surrounded by colourful trees
Shaking its fragrant branches
In the middle of the pool
Coming from the depths
The light of life!

As I approached the light
Under the miraculous rain
An extraordinary well-being
It took over me
From the tiptoes
To the root of the hair
Free from all curse
Of the wicked witch

I was puffed with stardust
Which wrapped me up sweetly.
In a blink of an eye
My love has appeared!

Now yes...
The idyllic frame
It's complete and happy
There is no shadow of pain!

WHEN SILENCE COMES

While my eyes moisten
I'm thinking
What can I do
If you don't love me anymore?
Nothing
I can't do anything!

Love cannot be forced
It flows naturally
I can't make you love me!

Silence came instead of thee
You don't have to say anything
Silence says more than a thousand words!

There will be something more eloquent?

RETURN TO CHILDHOOD

I returned
And when I came back
The first thing I did
It was to drop the bags
And to go to sip
The places of my childhood
I couldn't be happier
Even the birdies seemed the same
Perhaps the fourth generation.

I was delighted with the figs
Black and juicy
Figs
Have always been my downfall
I stuck myself in the brambles
I harvested a handful
Of very ripe blackberries
I had scratched my arms
Hands and mouth tinted black
Do you believe I was happy?
That moment
Wasn't the 65-year-old woman
That was there
But the 10-year-old child
Living joyful and free
Inside of me.

I ran across the field
I caught a bunch of daffodils
And some bells
I always liked these flowers
I was surprised
We were in the end of summer
And still daffodils!
Anyway, there must be
With climate change
Everything is changing!

I looked at the lush thriving tree
That stood in front of me
I was really amazed
From the tall oak
Standing so firm
So rooted and strong
With beautiful protective branches
For all the little birds
It reminded me
My parents' house
My beacon and my shelter.

It was time to go home
The fireplace was lit
It was October
But it was already cold
I settled in
On the cozy old armchair
I put the blanket on my legs
And I let me relaxing

Hearing the crackle of ash wood
Looking absorbed through the flames
With a sated and washed soul
In good memories.

Sweetness for the heart!

WHEN THE DEPARTURE APPROACHES

I knew this day was coming
As much as we postpone
The departure is inevitable
The supposed postponement
Is just a mental illusion
Because physically
Time is marking
An inexorable measure
To which none of us
Can escape
However
We do not know what day
The time decides
Not to give us more time.

Sometimes time
Takes us by surprise
And gives us the checkmate
Like someone who gives a fulminating blow
Just a few seconds of discomfort
And we plunge
Into a blue sea of tranquility
Others, it is like a gentle breeze
That refreshes and soothes us
And we are transferring ourselves smoothly
Like someone who drinks a delicious drink

In small sips
It is what is called a holy death
It's good to have the backpack always ready.
Others, however,
Time makes us suffer painfully
Every fibre of our being
As if it were harsh and macabre revenge
The pains are so unbearable
That we cry out all the time for the reaper
But deep down
We don't want to see it
Nor do we want it painted!

They have to learn
To endure the pain
By making their own morphine
Although it seems strange
Impossible or unbelievable
The truth is we will better overcome
The toughness of the fight
With acceptance and self-control.

I believe the strength of the spirit
Well based on good moral values
Such as
Altruism, sharing, detachment
In strong feelings
Such as
Joy, love, gratitude
Are fundamental stones
To help us cross the stream
To the other bank!

AS GOD WANTS

I am a simple woman
Who tries to open my way
And go in peace
Looking for...

It doesn't matter anymore
Whatever comes from now
Are blessings
Gifts
To sweeten my life
Kisses
Hugs
Soft swinging
Magic ribbons
That will bond love
And rock me sweetly!

Life is an act of love ...

I'll move on
Calm and serene
As long as God wants!

I WILL MISS MY SEA

I will miss my sea
Oh yeah, it's my sea
I got used to seeing it as mine
So great the proximity
And the heat that unites us
So many outbursts
Of sadness and joy
So many wise advice
So much guidance given
When I cried or when I laughed
The departure time
Approaches quickly
Come dressed in velvet
With satin bows.

There's a tightness in my heart
So many years of familiarity...

I end the last boxes
Pretty boxes
With painted stars and hearts
Where I keep my memories
So grateful to my soul
The breeze from the sea
Loaded with smells and laughter
And the seashells
Formed by each tear shed

For each emotion felt, a seashell
Sadness, joy, despair, relief
Fear, dare, ingratitude
warmth, understanding
Friendship and love
I only left on the beach
The shells of hatred and grudge
Next ebb
They will be taken
To the bottom of the sea!

I gather all the seashells
In the same box
The bad ones will soften
With proximity
From the shell of love
The one of joy is anxious
To give them a big hug.

I got a message from the ocean waves
I hope you are very lucky in your old future.

Looking through the bedroom window
I see the immense sea
Blowing kisses to me
Looking through the lounge window
I see the garden
Full of the flowers I planted
I feel like they're sad for me
They know
I won't be back!

I can't describe in words
The amalgam of feelings and emotions
That's ploughing inside me
I don't know if it's joy
For going back to what I left
If it's sadness
Not seeing my flowers again smiling
And the uncertainty of not knowing
If I will see again
This sea caressing my feet
Hugging and kissing my whole body
Or simply
If we'll be looking at each other again
I, sitting at the water's edge
Letting me captivate
By the passionate whispers of the waves
It will be a mixture of all this
And just for that
I don't know how to decipher what I feel
I just know, I will miss my sea!

I'M IN LOVE WITH YOU

Wrapped in your manly and beloved arms
I finish my last wills.

I'm on the verge
Of leaving for the last abode
I've always been in love with you
You did everything
To make me joyful and happy
Another thing, love
I couldn't wait from you
Once more and for the last time I tell you.

Life is not always fair and fair should be
Badly spoken words
Can cause much suffering
Oh and go back, it's already impossible
Going further, darling, is a difficult task
Xylophone stood back there
Forgotten in childhood
Where I played so many times, full of hope
In a blessed and loving future
I still hope to live that dream...
A thousand years from now?
Two thousand maybe?
Love, we will be happy, now or in eternity!

Because I'm very much in love with you

Hearing about love melts my heart
Laugh, give me your hand, sing with joy
All I want is for you to be happy
No illusion and pain, honey, trust me!

OUR NAVEL

I found a dewy flower
I named it the pearl of life
The dewdrop refracted the sunlight
And the flower was so beautiful
It was my rainbow
I looked at her with delight
It gave me so much satisfaction
I didn't want to lose her
I kept her in a glass bell jar
To be able to contemplate her.

I was happy
And I was so satisfied
That I didn't even notice
That she was dying
Only when she died
I realized
I only cared about me.

Now I wonder
How could I be so selfish?

No one is happy
With selfishness as the cornerstone
Helping each other
Happiness is more lasting
And every corner of our being

Will be filled with joy and lull.

I know that many times
We don't do it for evil
We live distracted
And we don't notice
In the suffering of others
Let's make an effort
To look around us...

Our navel
It's in good health!

BURSTING FROM THE RUBBLE

The roof collapsed on my head
It wasn't just any roof
The load was too much
Such are the cruelties of life
I long held the fear
It could collapse any moment
Fearing its descent on me
What would become of me?
What I feared happened
I was trapped under tons
Of reinforced concrete
Lying all smashed up
Panic was coursing
Every fiber of my being
Could I emerge from the rubble?
As the river of blood
Increased its flow
With amazing mental gymnastics
I managed to retain
The last drop of blood
And it was that last drop of blood
That rescued me from death.

Staggering, but determined to get up
I struggled to the sea
I sat on the water line
And let the waves

Kiss my whole body
Miraculous kisses
That restored my strength
I am grateful to life
That gave me the opportunity
To be just me
From now on!

Epilogue:

Good always wins, strength overcomes weakness.
Mental strength leads us to overcome the greatest
difficulties. It means, we must never give up, even
in extreme situations, miracles can happen.
But don't forget, the biggest slice of effort is yours!

THE SMILE OF YOUR EYES

While I slept beside thee
I looked at you
Absorbed by tranquility
Of your expression
Focused on your eyelids
Full of lashes
Through your imperceptible
Eye movement
I travelled
Through your winged dreams!

The beauty of that wings
Captured my attention.

They were woven in fine silk
Finished with gold thread
And dotted with Swarovski crystals
The fluttering
Of such sumptuous wings
Made the most beautiful
Melody sound
While distributing a divine dream
To the soul and heart.

A scented smile of red roses
Appeared on your lips
Ecstatic

I continued to look at you.

I lost track of time
Because time stopped
So that I could absorb without haste
The delicious fragrance
That emanated from your dream
Lost happily in this sea of emotions
I reached the climax with your awakening
A sublime smile played in your eyes
The warmth of that smile
Made me boil.

And I danced Kizomba
In the smile of your eyes
In the lap of your lips
Tired and happy
I surrendered to the beauty of thy heart!

LOVING IS WONDERFUL

(Translated from Portuguese sonnet)

I rode my beautiful workhorse
I left with elegance, galloping around the
world
I quickly relieved myself of all the stuff
I woke up from my heavy and deep sleep!

In the dungeons of the depths, I left
All bad pain and disbelief
I give thanks to God for having loved who I
loved
The disagreements are over forever!

It is wonderful to love and be loved ...
I'm happy because I found my beloved
It is important and valuable while it lasts!

I will do everything to make it last forever
It's pampering love and live in the present
Living with joy, not bitterness!

SHOULD BE

I don't agree
With these
World days
Of this and that!
I think
Every day
Should be
A world-wide day
Of everything!

Father
Mother
Children
Grandparents
Grandchildren
Children's
Trees
Water
Elderly
Smile
Kiss
Hug
Dog
Cat
Thank you
All!

Should be...

AND MY MISTAKE WAS BELIEVING

And my mistake was believing
Believe that you wanted me
Believe you loved me
Believe that without me, you couldn't live
Believing that I was the air you breathed
Believe that without me, you would die
And I didn't want to see you suffer ...
Believe that I could rely on you
Believe in your love, sworn eternally
Believing in complicity
And in the magic between us
That I believed it would be forever
And so many times you told me
I will love you forever, my dear
Nothing will make me stop loving you!
You are the sun illuminating my life
I will love you forever
I love you and I don't know why!
After swears and swears of love
I believed in you
But what!
I forgot that forever
Is a long time!

You sent me to hell
And here I am, waiting for you
Sitting at the door of it

I waited, I waited ...
Not knowing what my crime was.
And I'm still waiting for you
With my heart in my lap
Adorned with promises and ivy
I remembered the old chants
Who by ivy passed and did not cut
His love did not remember
I thought I was wrong at the address
This hell you sent me to
It's the one on the longing street
Right next to the Police Station?!

Out here it is cold to crack
I'm going to meet you
And we love each other elsewhere
Mild, calm, in the moonlight
Where you can hear our heartbeat
The devil heard my thought
He opened the bolts and tricked me
I thought I was going to meet you
Towards Nirvana
The sly tricked me
It took me on another path
Bad track record
Landed in ancient Eden
With coiled snakes
On the trunks of loaded apple trees
Of bright red apples.

-Eat, they are yours

You can eat every morning.

I knew I couldn't eat
I knew they were heresies
I wanted to come to you
And fall asleep in your arms.

-Eat, they are yours!

Satan tried me again

-Eat, they are yours!

And in the third one, I couldn't resist
I swirled through seas and moons
And only then I saw that I lost you
I returned to the door of hell
In the eagerness to find you
Here I am, sitting on a rock
Waiting for you
But please come on a winter day
 Inside is hot
And my mistake was
Believe in you, my love!
The devil took me
On overseas paths
For directions I didn't want
And my mistake was believing
I would be happy with you!

PASSWORD – Live Life

Oh life suffered
Why should we suffer in this life?
I pricked my heart
In one of the ramblings at sunset
The thorn was hidden amid the roses
I was reckless and clumsy
The night fell quickly
Despite the moonlight
I moved away from the rose bushes
For not offering security
I was deceived by overconfidence
The lush branch
Exerted a strong attraction on me
Trusting blindly, it's a big mistake
My heart keeps bleeding
Slowly...
I start feeling calm and relaxed.

A spark of light
Lit up my brain for seconds
I urgently needed to react
The calm and relaxation I was feeling
It was due to the lack of blood
That dripped from my body
More and more empty
I ripped the shirt I wore into strips
I bandaged my chest

Sat on the floor against the wall
And called 112.
I grabbed life by the collars
I kicked death
Help came quickly
If today I'm still alive and in good health
It was due to the speed
With which I took advantage
Of the spark of light
That lit up my brain for seconds.

Live life!

The slogan that was briefly
On my retina
Reacting is crucial
Never let ourselves be overwhelmed
By the circumstances.

We can change the needle
From the train of our life
Or to prevent derailment
Or to change the destination of the trip!
We must keep our eyes wide open
For any of the situations
In order to avoid accidents
And there are so many accidents
In this life!

BEFORE AND AFTER

I feel the light my enemy
I live the days and nights
In the same darkness
I'm exhausted from so much fighting
And I don't even have tact in my hand
I can't feel
The good if it still exists
I can't see
My myopia persists
Of the five senses
Which one do I have left
It is a myopic vision
The touch wrinkled
Smell is covered
It is an illusion to hearing
So...
My body sucks
And the soul that remains
I can't find whiteness
Of the child who died

After all who am I?
Why so much torture
I just know
Someone not born has died!

I lack the arabesques

To draw my thought
But what does it matter now?
If the inside of me
I already feel encouragement
Writing appeases me
It transmits me so calm
Before the poem so much bitterness
And then?
Oh now I feel so white
Like a source of pure water.

GOGYOHKA

I walk afraid
through the dark forest
I'm dropping scarlet flowers
As by a miracle
I feel more confident and secure!

~

One day
You will find
What you have always wanted
Or maybe not...
You might find a lot better!

THE EMBRACE OF THE BRAMBLES

When we are abandoned
Even the embrace of the brambles
Provides comfort.

I went to meet a monument
Called Alminha
On the commendations path
It was not easy to reach it
because of the jungle that I had to face.
I skipped brambles
I crouched down so I could pass.
There's a will there's a way
I reached the goal
After suffering a lot.

Imposing and upright
Embraced by the brambles
Loaded with blackberries
Sweet juicy fruit.
But what's the use
If he can't eat them!
It hurt me to see the thorns
On his stone spiked
We cannot count the hours
Of such great suffering
It's like a sloppy dog
Without an owner.

There are pains that soothe
Mistreatment and abandonment
When we feel them
Like a hug.

This *Alminha*
Defied scorching summers
Winds and storms
Passing from century to century
But resisted
Facing oblivion
With faith and hope
That someone who loves culture
And heritage
Give it back its importance!

It's us
Inattentive and hurried individuals
That we hasten death
Of the legacies of our ancestors
With contempt and neglect
With which we treat them.
Oh absent-minded people
Heart insensitive
Stonier
Than the monument's granite.
Let's roll up our sleeves
And take care of our cultural heritage
Giving it life so it can avenge
For all eternity!

LOVE LIFE DEATH

(Poetry Elfchen)

Love
A feeling
In my heart
As a sweet throb
Life!

Life
A blessing
If no life
Nothing matters at all
Death!

Death
Life's absence
End of everything?
Buried corpse, free soul
Eternity!

MY BOYFRIEND FOREVER

My friend, my lover, my mate
I love and respect you and always will be
Last stronghold, my whole world!

I surrendered to the complicity
That brought us together
Your tender and different way of being
Captivated me
I beautified myself for you
With lilies and tenderness
Breathing and dreaming life with thee
Is an adventure
In the hope of the sun
That warms and enlightens me
To dare and believe tomorrow
Is a shower of glitter!

Nothing or nobody will change my mind
Loving you was the best thing in my life
My dear, my eternal boyfriend
Where life with you
Will be an eternal odyssey
It remains to say
That the mission of making you happy is mine
I learned to love you
In the magic of your words
Sweetness

That forever held my soul to yours
Wherever you are
I will trust ya, my love!

THE CLOUDS IN MY EYES

The sky is clear
Not a single cloud
Stains the wonderful azure.

Where did the clouds go?

I grab a mirror
And I see the clouds in my eyes.

Where is the love I loved so much?

The clouds in my eyes
They won't let me see him
Will someday
My eyes be clear?

Hope remains at my side
Because I want to see again
Who I loved so much
And I still love!

In my eyes
A flash of joy!

I look into my heart
And I see it spotted
Of nostalgia ...

THE MOST POWERFUL HEALING

Love
Is the most powerful healing
So
Why do people
Try hate and spite?

The world
Should be
Compassion and faith
Love and gratitude
Not war and hate.

I open my arms
I thank the Creator
The breath of life
That still holds me
Thank you, my Lord!

IT'S AUTUMN

I hide in autumn
Confident
In the polychromatic leaf's fall
Trying to find some warmth
The place is as cold as ice.

I lie down on the bed
of leaves painted by time
Longing that polychrome
Refreshes and sweetens my dreams
And I wake up smiling.

I pull the blanket
Made of loneliness
Sewn with meek thread
Bordered with ingratitude
But the feet don't get warm
And I can't sleep.

I will wait for a turnaround
May my heart warm ...

It's autumn
Woe...
There is still so much time
For summer coming!

BETWEEN THE SWORD AND THE WALL

Oh, mom, nobody wants me
Nobody accepts me
Everyone rejects me
I want to go to Rehab
There I will have someone
To take care of me.

This said so
It's a lump in the throat
A punch in the stomach
A revolt that revolves the insides.

Being schizophrenic is not sweet pear.

You blame yourself
Because you turned her world around
You changed her routine
Without thinking about the consequences
Didn't you think?
You were forced to separate from her
To take care
Of your old and sick parents
Your mother is sweet
Your father is a well of selfishness
She had hope and confidence
On the mother's protective wing.

But she is my daughter
And she can always count on me
Unconditionally
For her, I move mountains
Break the path
I do everything
And much more
There are several obstacles and friction
I am between the sword and the wall
Or I take care of my daughter
Or I take care of my parents.

For now the situation
Was tacked
I didn't have to choose
But I know
That the basting can burst
God is generous and merciful
Always worth me
In difficult times
Will not forsake me

Thank you, my Lord!

LOVING AND NOT BEING LOVED

Nostalgia
Thought
Tears
Suffering
One more year
This time sad and lonely
I went back twelve months
And I saw joy
Hope
Company
Confidence!

I was happy…

But now I know
That it was all illusion
Whom I loved so much
Played with my heart
Swore eternal love
And I naively believed
Sent me to hell
Only then did I wake up!

Left on me, injuries and sequels
This cursed love
I feel insecure
Attached by the devil

How do I know now
If they tell me the truth?
You don't know
It's a long shot
Of suffering
You already had your dose
Loving and not being loved is hard
Live your freedom
Don't let them bother you!

I WOULD LIKE TO BE

(Translated from Portuguese sonnet)

I wanted to be nightingale or lark
Flying nonstop through space
To bring you peace and joy
The tenderness of my good and sweet embrace.

I wanted to be the honey, fruit or flower
I wanted so much to be nature
So that you oh, my dear love
Would have me at your table forever!

Wanted to be dahlia or allegory
I wanted to be a warm breeze on a cold night
I wanted to be the lowland and the meadow!

I wanted to be the sea and the mountain
So you would see the great longing
From my joyful and happy girl time!

MYSTIC

(Acrostic)

More and more I'll love you

Yet, this sentiment cannot be bigger

Sweet , enigmatic, mystic

Thus an exotic and exquisite mix

In perfect serenity and abstraction

Come, my angel, I'm here for you!

I LOVE YOUR GAZE

I love your gaze ...
Even plunged into sadness
Your eye look has charm!

Your gaze is absolutely charming!

It has magic and attraction ...
I let myself sink into the clear waters
Unique from thy mysterious source!

Your gaze is absolutely charming
Beautiful as a polished stone's shine
Is there anything more wonderful?
Oh dear, I've said it a million times
I reaffirm my love, until the end of life!

MAESTRO

I hear the rain
Falling vigorously on the roof
And together with the wind
Whipping the church's glass panes
The noise is scary
Maestro arrives
To conduct the orchestra
One by one
People are leaving the place
Maestro
Is hardworking and competent
But the audience
Says that music is downright bad
The music is not bad
It is true that musical taste
Is variable
But the audience abandoned the recital
To the first chords
Because they ran away in fear
Of the storm
They shielded themselves
From an infamous lie
It is easier to use the lie
Than taking on their weaknesses.

It is necessary to use the goodwill
In everything, we intend to do

The ill will
It will lead us to failure.
Worst of all neither is the fact
Of not having succeeded
Accomplishes what we intended
But extreme fatigue
That stays in our body and spirit
Anything done with goodwill
Has a chance to be successful
We need lightness
And success in our lives
Because there is nothing impossible
There are things
More difficult than others
The problem
Is that we often settle down.

Today I became knowing
Of an extremely inspiring case
A 75-year-old man
Completed a law degree
It was a youth dream
But at that time
There was no opportunity to achieve it
There were other priorities in his life
Such as
The education of his children
His dream was only postponed
It's never late
To make our dreams come true
If we leave them forgotten on the shelf

It's our fault
We lacked courage, determination
Commitment and dedication
All of these elements are part of
Goodwill package
That we left abandoned in a corner
When we settled down
After we have made up
A thousand and one excuses.

That 75-year-old man
Certainly
Didn't want to take the course
To apply his knowledge
In the world of work
But rather as enrichment
Personal and intellectual
This is so rewarding
Personally
I know some inspiring cases
I'm remembering
From a brilliant young maestro
Full of talent
And from a reputable lawyer
It's a happiness
To be able to taste the fruits
Of worthy achievement
And the fruits are not all the same
We can choose the ones we like best
It is not mandatory to eat the same
The taste is eclectic

There are inspiring cases
Because they fought
Our case can also be inspiring
Excuses for what?

JUST POET

(Translation from Portuguese sonnet)

I sense and even hear behind me
The laugh of scorn of those who make fun
I keep walking my way
What they say or do, it doesn't matter.

And only the soul I want to dress
With rich shiny brocades
The top priority is my feeling
Well, let them snort and snarl between teeth!

I'm not crazy and much less silly
What's inside me is what counts
Everything else is sweet, a light breeze!

Love, well wish, in the world is rare
Respect and goodwill are scarce
And I am just a simple poet!

YOU ARE MY SONNET

(Translation from Portuguese sonnet)

You in my life, you are the cornerstone
You came out of nowhere to love you
And I haven't felt for a long time
Oh, this great love, which I so wanted!

You arrived like a sweet hurricane
You touched my heart deep
You cast the anchor, you tied the rope
You picked up the basket, we picked
blackberry!

And so this beautiful love was born
Gone are the days of temerity
I will love you with great fervour!

A shining sun was born in the soul
Illuminating this happiness
With you, hand in hand forever!

EXCRUCIATING SUFFERING

Prostrate in bed
Unable to move
A truck
Had passed over me
I was all smashed
It spared my heart
For what I want this sad life
In this excruciating suffering?

I looked inside myself
I watched what was left
The heart full of love
I scolded myself severely
Don't blaspheme
The best of you is left
Raise your hands
And thank the Creator!

A RAY OF SUNSHINE

A ray of sunshine
Penetrated the dark cloud.
The dark cloud
Burst into tears
As it was hit
By the ray of sunlight.
The fields, trees and flowers
Thanked it.

It rained night and day non-stop.

A deluge was feared
For the crimes of humanity.
The cloud took time to calm
It was the thunder
To put it in its place.

Now
Without any modesty
And animosity
The sun shone with happiness
And the cloud sang a song.
Down on Earth,
The flowers smiled
Filling nature
With perfume and colour.
The trees sensually swayed
Their branches
In a greeting of love!

WE DO NOT FORGET

I read somewhere

We do not give up on what we want.
We give up on what hurts.

Truth!

Not because we want
But because it hurts a lot

No one likes to live the evil
No one wants to be a punching bag
It remembers us of the flail on the threshing
floor
Striking the cereal
No, we do not forget ...

It stays right there in the background
We do not look
Time eventually leads the pain
And what stays
It's a sweet and soft memory.

Time is a still
Distilling the pain
Until it turns white!

I NEED TO LOVE SOMEONE

When I get to a place
In search of great love
I'm already leaving
Why this constant stubbornness
In being friends with life
If I only find pain in it!

I need to love someone ...
But there is a claw
Well curved
That cuts me down and oppresses me
Why they treat me with disdain
If my soul is so sublime.

I say I love everyone
That I find along the road
Why do they tear my belly
And abandon me gutted?

I go in search of love ...
Walking the adventure trail
I don't know anything about his whereabouts
But I will find him
Even if I go around the whole world!

I want happiness
Everybody wants...

But not everyone sees it
What I really want
It's just, don't forbid me anything!

HAIKU

A tear fell from my eye
But the smile
Picked it up on lap!

~

Penetrate my core
And I will give you
My most beautiful smile!

~

Because smiling enlightens me
And help me to walk
And this way is happiness!

~

Innocence
The purest form
Of loving!

THE SIX TIPS

An angel gave me six tips to find love
Symphony, dream, hope
Moon, sand, desire.

I filled my backpack with hope
And when the sun came up
I left in search of love.

Someone told me he lived on the moon.

I walked under the hot sun
The scorching sand
Burned the soles of my feet
At sunset I rested under a pink magnolia
I looked at the sky
Contemplate the moon
It was still so far away ...
The desire to find love was so great
That I let myself be rocked by the dream
Governed by the wonderful symphony
Of a flock of hummingbirds.

I woke up with the lips of my love
Perched on mine!

MY TRANQUILLIZER

Why do I write?
Good question
I've been writing for so many years
That for me
It is a necessity like breathing.

Writing
Soothes my inner demons
Reassures me
Makes me reflect
Is my tranquillizer
And consequently
Improves me as a human being.

Writing
Mainly poetry
Is the elaborate sap
That circulates in my veins
An additive to my blood
Taking strength
Courage
And lots of sweetness
To all parts of my being.

Writing
Bring me closer to God
And enables me

The ability to dream
With a better world
A very round world
Without sharp edges.

It is in the laps that the world takes
That it will be chiseling
It is in the turns that life takes
That we build ourselves!

It's all in our hands
God wants us to be happy!

IT'S ETERNAL

Today, I wanted to disappear
I wanted a UFO to catch me
And take me far away
Where I could cry alone
No one to see
Without anything to make me suffer
Where I could live
In light and peace
In perfect harmony!
And about love?
I think, I think, I think ...
It's hard to believe
Doubts arise
But not because I love thee!

I make a huge effort
And I wonder
Why someone
Would give me love
If all life
They only gave me pain!

I wish I was born
With some gifts ...
But I was born only with defects
In sadness, I invented joy
To be able to do magic

Now…
On the threshold of my winter
The last season of life
I just need a roof
Where I feel protected
Where nothing hurts me
It doesn't matter
Whether it is in heaven or in hell
But I know very well
That the love I feel for thee
It's infinite, it's unconditional
It's eternal!

A SEA OF SOLITUDE

Words are blunt
They hurt like daggers
Tears come to the eyes
But don't fall
They are supported by the strength
That comes from within
I spread the sheets
Bordered with tolerance
In the waves of patience
That rock me sweetly.

I lie down
Close my eyes
And rest.

I can't let myself be hurt
By sharp words
In the stone of arrogance
There are people
Who are born and die
Without having learned to be kind.

Rest, I offered to myself
Will restore the energy sucked
By the negativism
Of unreasonable words
Once again

A gesture of love
Was trampled underfoot.
There are still people
Who despise love
There are still people
That is governed
By the baton of egocentrism.

Where does selfishness
Arrogance and ingratitude take us?

No doubt
To a cold and uncomfortable bed
No doubt
To a sea of solitude.

TIME AND LIFE

Oh, Time, stop the stopwatch
And let Life live
Do not take everything in front of you
See, who you let suffering
You run like crazy
And Life is falling behind
Where does your rush take you?
If you do not see poetry at all!
Open your eyes, Time
Walk slower
Let Life enjoy the moment
You're running so hard
She barely has time to love!

Oh, Time, be more complacent
Walk slower
Time, what do you want the time for?
If you are losing lives one by one
So many times ...
We don't know how to choose the signs
Whose fault is it?
Of life?
Of time?
Mine or yours?
Or both?
If I could stop time
I would travel in an ox cart!

I would like to be a gold digger
Sifting gravel
Separate the gold
But there are so many times
That I just screw up
Then I'm regretting
Missed opportunities
Pains and regrets crying
And lived joys
That I had judged eternal
But they never come back!
Whose fault is it?
Of life?
Of time?
Mine or yours?
I just know
That I love you more and more!

YOKE - domestic violence

I made the crossing of the burning desert
I burned the soles of my feet
In the scorching sand
In the desert of my life
Under the torrid sun and thin air
I felt faint.

I swallowed the cacti
That calmed my thirst
But they tore my mouth
And they made my heart bleed.

I don't give up easily
Maybe I'm crazy
Exhausted I move on
Praying the rosary I keep in my hand.

I was hungry for love and affection
I was cold
Without a kiss to wrap me up
I fell asleep without a hug
To rest my head
But anyway...
I don't give up on living.

I look ahead and what do I see?
A deep black hole

Where fear thickens
And in cold sweats, it condenses
But anyway...
I walk straight ahead
Towards my destiny!

I burst with courage
The chain links
You tied me up
To your bland and depressing life
Not a plea
Not a complaint
Only to God I prayed!

Today I no longer carry the yoke on my neck
And the halter, I burned it
At the fire of my dowry!

A NEW OPPORTUNITY

Today the sun rose at 05:56am
Upon waking
I felt like watching the sunrise!

A dense mass of clouds
Covered the sky
And failed my expectations
But I don't give up
Because I know that tomorrow
I have a new opportunity
Unless my life
Be interrupted
But I never think about it
If I think my life
Can stop at any time
Inhibits my imagination
My creativity
And the faculty of execution
Are compromised
I waste time
And time is so valuable!
And I love life so much
Or in the smallest things
Or in the grandest phenomenon
In fact...
Life is a succession of greatness!

I open my arms
And I thank for what I am
For the affections that make me happy
And for the part of the world
That belongs to me.

Tomorrow...
I will have a new opportunity!

IT WAS DAWN

(Acrostic)

In the depths of my heart
Today, I found a tiny pink pebble.

Where have you been, my love?
Always I'm aware of your presence...
So, I know you were within me!

Darling, the tiny pink pebble I found
Always will be from now on, my amulet
Whenever you enter inside my heart
Never go away without the day dawn!

THE MIRROR

I walk my way
Filled with mistakes
Dreams, losses and damages
I had believed it was happiness
Walking beside me
But again
I have to sing my "fado"
Sad, lonely song
Doleful strains of suffering
I would rather have a "Corridinho"
To give colour and joy
And shake my life!

God, my good Father
Hear my prayer
Put someone in my way
For I fear and don't want loneliness
Send me one
To take my hand
Love me with much love
With desire and passion
I need someone to love
Let me not waste
The love in my heart
Growing, blooming and overflowing.

Father, what was my sin?

Help me to understand
I'm tired of the burden
That I carry on my shoulders
The weight is too much
Download at every step
I rest so I can continue
I glimpse happiness
Leagues away
But for this walking
Loaded like a pack animal
I won't have time to get there.

So, Divine Father
Lighten my load
For rest and happiness
Until my death.

I look in the mirror of time
And I see a face charred by pain
With deep grooves from crying
The complexion is undefined and brownish
Of thirsty affection
I see there written
Pains that I remembered
Strange marks I didn't know
From the heartache
This is and was my lot.

Oh, Lord, my Father
I don't trust
My gold plated mirror

I can't be so mistreated
Heavenly Father, lend me Yours.
I want to take a look ...
Eureka!
I see a pure, fresh and beautiful face
There is nothing ruined!

Then my Lord spoke:

What you're seeing
In the mirror of truth
Is your ornate soul
Lined with pearls and diamonds
Wreathes like rainbows
An offering
For having suffered from the stones
That life has unfairly given you!

IT'S TIME

I walk the inhospitable paths
Of my existence
I don't even know why I insist
In the face of so much adversity
Father, my stay here
No longer makes sense
Life showed that for me
There is no happiness.

I had dreams and wishes
Like anyone else
I ran after them
But grab them
I didn't succeed in this life
Surrendering to my uselessness
But I don't want to live idly
I really wanted to be happy
But I was deluded
Deceived and betrayed.

God, my Father
I thank you for the life You gave me
But now wake up
Because I think you fell asleep
You know my time
Here on Earth, it ran out.

Now I know it's time
To return to the eternal home
Without looking at ideology
Race or colour
My verb was to love
I look up at the sky
And I thank those who loved me!

WHO AM I?

Who am I?
Poet
Dreamer
Lover
Thinker
Hiker
Rebel
Romantic
Misunderstood
Revolutionary
Clumsy
True
Active
Frontal
Azure
Earth
Sea
Thorn
Rose
Support
Wheat field
Hobby
Poppy rippling in the wind?

Only
A human being
That likes to be

Dreamer
Lover
Poet!

The rest, just
Artifice
Appendix
Accessory
Ornaments
String
Ribbons
Silk
Lace
To tie the bouquet!

NOBLE FATE

Destiny wanted me
To come face to face
With evildoers.

Destiny wanted me
To help those
Who hurt me.

Destiny wanted me
To give flowers to
Whoever insulted me!

Destiny wanted me
To kiss those
Who betrayed me.

Destiny wanted me
To put everything
Behind my back.

Destiny wanted me
To give priority
To affection.

Destiny wanted me
To fulfil
The normal law of life.

Destiny wanted me
To continue being a caregiver
At a new stage.

Destiny wanted me
To be blessed
With such great grace.

Destiny wanted
To lay bare
The truth of reality.

That's what destiny ordained.

Thank you, my Lord
For such
A noble fate!

LONGINGLY

I miss you so much
That longing drowned my heart
So many truths
That I hold in my hand
I wish my hand could open
And throw them in the wind
That he might carry them
Even unto thee
And you could see my great torment!
But what would I gain from tormenting you
And making cry your beautiful eyes
If what I just want is to remind you
I never stopped loving ya!

You left...
And my eyes were hurt
Looking at the line that borders on infinity
Oh, there were so many my appeals
That bumped into the walls of my scream!

And time went slow
And you didn't come ...
In my heart
I was waiting for your coming
I dreamed that one day
You would come back
Secretly...

I nurtured that hope
It was unconscious
I loved you so much
But you never knew ...
The dream collapsed
Hope died
I stopped looking at the line
That touches infinity ...
Now I look at the cypress
That was always in front of me!

MY SEA

I love this sea
I'll say farewell to him
And maybe see him
For the last time...

How am I going to live
Without my sea?
Without his kisses
Sent in the sea breeze
With seaweed smell
And round pebbles
Remembering my breasts
When I was a girl
Round, smooth and firm
The erosion of time
It's relentless
I am not afraid
It's necessary to know
How to accept ageing
I'm not that girl anymore
With firm and satin shapes
But I'm a woman
Now ripe and sweet
Sweet and tender
Already with wrinkled skin
But so sweet and juicy!

Now, I'm a woman
Ripe and sweet ...
So sweet and juicy!

I love this sea
In thought
I sail on his waves
I'm heading for the sea
Maybe for the last time
To give him my last kiss!

STICKS, STONES AND WORDS

Hey you there
That judged me
Arrogantly and boastfully
Who do you think you are?
How dare you contest
My words of peace and love?
I'm a poet
I can use my creativity
And powerful imagination
To express me
Like a mirror that reflects
The values I defend and preserve
For the common good of humanity
Using for this purpose
Allegories and metaphors
Or other style figures.

The values
That I try to defend and preserve
They will make you
 Have a better life too
Just like your children
Grandchildren, great grandchildren
I defend and will always defend
A fairer and more balanced society
Where all of us and generations to come
May be happy

When you say categorically
That I'm linked to the devil forces
That my words tend to cause harm
When you tell me to shut up
When you forbid me
To say another word
When you impose me silence
What is the force that moves you?
What right do you tell me to shut up?
With what right do you stop me
To spread love and peace around the world?
Without a single reference
Like an inflated balloon
With false self-righteousness
No healthy motivation
What a small mind!

Do you know the difference between us?
I carry in my arms
Bunches of poems
Tied with roses of all colours
That leave my hands
Divinely scented!
People like you
Carry weapons in their arms
And the smell of your hands
Are gunpowder and death!
The world is full of enemies
Trolls, hackers and fanatics.
What would become of the world
If there were no poets?

It would be certainly
Darker and harsher!

To the viperine tongues
Who hide behind fake profiles
I advise them to be honest
Yet...
They make me feel pity
They are poor in spirit
Who wander like lost souls
And as such, they need our prayers
For them, I ask God
To shed light on their path
So they can see the terrain they step on
In order not going bumping around.

I finish my poem
Humbly using
The words of Jesus
When evildoers
Nailed Him to the cross.

Father forgive them, they don't know what they do.

BEWILDERMENT

(Acrostic)

Be mine and I will be all yours
Ever and ever for all eternity
Why are you delaying to dwell
Inside my cosy and tender being?
Living this way, a great and marvel love
Darling, you are everything I need
Ethereal love will end my bewilderment
Realm of my sweet paradise.
My dear, no words to express my affection
Ever and ever I will be all yours
Nothing at all will stop me
To love you for all eternity!

HAIKU

Without love
What matters
To live?

~

Come share my smile
And together
We will sow love!

~

If you allow me
I will be balm and bonanza
In your body and in your soul

THE NEXT DAY

My life
Is punctuated by faith
For hope
For love
That I put in everything
I believe
That there will always be
One more day
To improve
To find
The way
The truth
Peace
The light!

I trust the next day
A day that is a gift
And will give me
The chance to do
What I didn't do
I always say
Tomorrow will be better
I'm in a hurry...
I know the day will come
The last day...
And there will be no more hurry
And there will be no more

The next day!

I'm not a robot
But I will try to comply
The mission
For which I was programmed!

MY CHEST'S JEWELLERY

(Translated from Portuguese quatrains)

So the verbs I like the most
It is undoubtedly the verb to love
Give serenity to my face
Because I'm always conjugating it.

Age is also seed
Because it gives tenderness to my gaze
The gesture becomes complacent
The walking is smoother.

In youth are ardours
In its corner accommodated
Forty years are glow
Of treasures so well kept.

And in my treasure chest
I have precious jewels
I don't have silver I have gold
I have no thistles I have roses

They are roses that were heritage
From so great and good friends
They are jewels of faith and hope
Oh, that I will bequeath to my children!

STANZAS OF 10 WORDS

Without you
My love
I am a broken wings birdie!

Honey
You are my bread and freshwater
In the desert!

My love
You are my breath
You are my sustenance!

You're the spice
That makes the difference
In my life!

You are my chili
My sweetness
My ground, my everything!

Our love
Is stronger than everything
And will live forever!

My heart's love
Flower of my path
My life's sun!

I'm addicted to your love
This addiction
Makes me happy!

I want
To be happy
The rest of my life!

My sweet love
I will love you
Forever and ever!

It is so surprising
Comforting and rewarding
To love you!

Sweetie,
Forever and ever and ever
Forever and ever together!

CHILDREN

Children!
Here in your journal
I leave hopes
I leave dreams
I leave heat
Shoulder unloading
My bag
Full of love!

Children look ahead...

Make the truth a gift
Even though the reality is harsh.

Because always love
Wins when we want ...
Be it, man or woman!

Child ...
It's crying and laughing
It is joy without wisdom

Child...
It's daybreak
It's a shining sun

Child...

It is seed that germinates
It is life that illuminates!

Child...
It is the dawn of hope
In this exile
Boys and girls
Don't tell my secret
I so wanted to be a child ...

I wanted so much!

TOPSY-TURVY

Everything is topsy-turvy
And me too
And it was through the back door
That I've heard about justice
I got a little sound in my ear
That justice was to give a chorizo
To whom gives a pig
It doesn't look bad ...
But is the chorizo good
Or is the pig poisoned?
Anyway
It seems to me that is here
The Devil's hand!

I continued down the alley
I landed on a path
A table set
A beautiful lace table towel
Gifts received as a gift
Some bread quarters
Two souls in prayer!

Suddenly
An evildoer wielding a sword
With a straight hit
Threw the bread in the trash
And something has never happened

Bread became vodka
The drunk had a party
But what a great shamelessness
A caption adorned his forehead!

-Injustice-

I found everything very strange
I was really confused
There is someone to explain to me
Because I don't understand anything
This is a big joke
Or a new fashion
Taking bread out of a poor man's mouth
Turn it into a bottle of vodka
And shove it down the throat
Of any drunk!

I remembered the stories
From John without fear
And Zé little people
That my grandpa told me.

I don't know if it's a man or a woman
Whether it's a cry or the creed
Or the house of horrors
Whether it's a pig or a chorizo
Save yourself if you can!

There are no more values
Justice was left homeless!

Is it a leaf or a bird?
I don't know!
I don't even want to know!
Everything's changed ...
Damn it
Everything to hell!

YOUR BLESSING, MY LORD

Today
I just want to thank
The life I still have
I count on your help
My God
To learn to fly ...

I leave behind
What I borrowed
Tied me up by depriving me
The freedom to be me ...
Now I'm free and confident
With what is genuinely mine!

I know it's not easy
Go back to being independent
I'm not afraid of challenges
I want to be autonomous
I want to feel like people!

Your blessing, my Lord!

DANCING WITH THE ENEMY

It dawns, dusks, dawns ...
And nothing changes, strictly nothing
Everything is frighteningly the same
I've lived with birds, fish and cats
A rattlesnake and a turtle
Hamsters and dogs
It was difficult to live with the rattlesnake
It was a stoic struggle
In permanent fear
Constantly alert
But fear strengthened me
And never made me give up
Don't even be quiet
Nobody understood
How could I live with such a company
For me, the most horrifying so far
In the beginning
It was a kind of enchantment
But that quickly broke
Then it was the struggle for survival
Nothing could distract me
Otherwise, I would die
And I was dancing the tango
With the enemy
At the sound of the rattle on the tail
Throughout my life
I was immunized against the constant stings

I always kept my chest open
Blunt marks on sores
Difficulty breathing and bleeding
Salivation and paralysis
And the anti-poison was always at hand
As a consequence, a heart disease
In my naivete
I wanted to tame the beast
I treated her with sponge cake
angel cakes and nun bellies cakes
But it wasn't worth it ...
There was no soul, neither big nor small!
She was cold-blooded
She didn't know gratitude
I doubt even that she had a heart.

After so many years
So many that I lost count ...
She tried to screw me with the lethal bite
The antidote had run out
I opened the door and put her in the street
Alone she was unable to survive
The burden, always on my shoulders
For me to solve everything
I was the picket on duty
But the blessed day has come
That I got tired of so much bite
When I opened the door, she disappeared
My heart got tight
I couldn't leave her abandoned
A year had passed

The animal became ill and mistreated
She already had nothing to eat.
If I didn't lay a hand on her
She ended up dying
Back at my house
She was calm and grateful
I found it so sweet
After all, she was a rattlesnake ...
Gradually it was revealing its nature
Cold, calculating and hard
Insurgent against me
With more impetus and wickedness
But anyway...
I played my part
I will not go into detail
It is too macabre and cruel
I thought I had made a pact with God
But it was with the devil!
The rattlesnake I loved
Returned to her kingdom, I know!

Always help those in need
Don't think of yourself
When you help someone
It is your enemies
Who need your help most
Your reward comes from God!

VAIN HOPE

I hold on to vain hope
In the illusion
That you still love me.

The illusion is sometimes good
Slowing up the suffering
While living in vain hope
I cherish hope
That I will not lose you!

Illusion...
It's a sweet feeling
It softens the pain!

There will be no suffering
When the illusion makes my eyes open!

Vain hope ...
It's not that bad
It's like a dove
Flowing in the morning
A feeling of purity and freedom
A flower in bloom!

While the illusion persists
I believe in your love!

THE I

There is so much that something
I don't even know what
Was distressing and tormenting me
But I couldn't find the reason
Because all the reasons seemed silly to me
Today by mere chance
And some controversy
I saw what bothered me so much
It was my I
That struggled within me
Tired of the prison where he lived
Caged inside the heart
No one deserves to live like this.

After all, that was it
Made in the cocoon of the heart
And the chrysalis
Was waiting for the metamorphosis
That always ends up happening
But I didn't even realize it
So big was my suffering
Only when I, already a butterfly
Was desperately flapping its wings
I opened the cage where I was enclosed
It streaked out like a rocket
No one likes to be badly loved
No one likes to be a plaything.

Without the I inside me ...
I felt empty light and free
Swinging on a jasmine branch
The I, went to the party, dressed in love
He was thirsty for freedom
He looked like a joyful and happy kid
Carried by the shoulders in a swing
Watching him dancing delighted me
It was truly exquisite
Before he left I gave him some advice
As if I could give advice ...

Behave like a true lord
Don't leash anyone
Measure your words well
Take the right measures
After uttered
If they are badly measured
They are excruciating open sores
Don't complain
Do not pray to Holy Engracia!
Never lose lightness, composure
Delicacy and lineage in the soul
What is nefarious is short-lived
Stay faithful and loyal with great courage.

I've done this all my life
But I wasn't rewarded
Also, reward not asked
If I have to love and be loved

It's not for the worldly possessions
But for what is inside me and you
Because otherwise
I don't want anything!

THE WRINKLES AND THE SMILE

Patiently
And without wavering
I go my way
My smile
Don't let me get discouraged.

My smile
Not always
It's a happy smile
Oftentimes
It's a sad smile
But anyway
And although full of pain
I never stopped smiling
Because smiling
Decreases pain
Decreasing the pain
I follow my path
Always forward
More lightly!

I look in the mirror
I see dimples
Smiling eyes
And sweet mouth
The smile
Is my reinforcement

I'm sure of that
Lights my eyes
And sweetens my mouth
Beautifies my face
And smooths out my wrinkles.

Oh, the wrinkles ...
Each groove an experience
A happening
One page
Of the great book
That life is
A story
Stuffed with adventures
Joys and pains
Loves and dislikes
Are part of life
Are part of our growth!

NEEDY WORLD

Today is deep cleaning day
I clean the dusty shelves
And the old silvers of my life
Already darkened
By the inexorable passage of time
I pulled the gloss
They were shining
They smiled with joy!

Silly
It wasn't the silver that smiled
It was you, reflected in them
Life is a mirror
It doesn't show you gold
If you wave silver
It doesn't show you bread
If you wave an empty hand.

I prepare to close this door
And open the one in front of me
What's beyond that door...
It is no longer totally unknown
Yet...
A lot of things happened there
The novelty does not scare me
I am fearless and curious
But what moves me the most
Is to know that behind that door

There is an affectionate
And needy world!

There are people waiting for me
There are people who are people!

There are lives that cross and move away
And meet again...
There are still dreams to live!
I want to help dream
I want to make dreams come true.

Dreams are ageless...

I live serenely and I still have dreams
Dreams never end
But my dreams now
It's dreaming the dreams of others
And make them happen!

There's still a long road ahead...

I want people to feel like people
And being people
It's having feelings
It's being able to get emotional
Light in the soul, love in the heart
We need to be supportive
Conscious, grateful
Charitable, benevolent
Caregivers

A clear self-portrait
Where there are no hidden cats
Not blurred vision
Just an overwhelming will
To make others happy
And when in others, it's who I love
My life makes perfect sense!

The wind blows gently
Taking and bringing love songs
It will be the same where I go ...

I give thanks to the Creator!

GOGYOHKA

What matters the rain, the cold
The snow and the wind outside
If within us shines the sun
That warms our heart
And gives light to our dreams!

~

Lean against my chest
And listen with fond
What my heart says...
It says you are the most
Beautiful constellation's star!

VIRTUAL FRIEND

Come, friend
Of all colours and quadrants
Come by land, come by air
Come by sea
Or simply walking
Come wherever you please!
But please
Don't bring with you
Infamous purposes
I am an honourable woman
Brings respect, fun and laughter
And let's sing and laugh
Till belly hurts!

I accepted you as a friend
Without ever asking you for anything
I opened the door and the window
I let you in my shelter
Painted blue watercolour
You sat and rested
And I, like a good hostess
I prepared you a great meal
That took me all morning!

Friendship cooked with goodwill.

In exchange for my hospitality
I just wanted your friendship
When you arrived
In tiptoes softly
You were affectionate
Sensitive and loving
And I was so touched
I even enjoyed your company
And I thought you loved poetry!

Suddenly everything changed
In the gentle waters of this river
A storm arose
When the real intent broke out
Your supposed friendship
It was weak, annoying and cold
You confused everything ...
You put your feet up for the boldness
And the charm is gone
Shrouded in the carnival!

A virtual friend
It may well be real
And nothing was like before
I just wanted to be your friend
And never your lover!

WHY WAS I BORN?

After all
Why was I born?

Simple.

A man and a woman lay themselves down
In a bond of love
He was for her
She was for him.

The spermatozoon met the egg
And they kissed
The making of me began.

After 9 months
I was ready to leave the dockyard.

I left through the vagina
It wasn't easy, it was a tough job
The place was tight
And the woman screamed a lot.

But I got out!

The woman smiled at me
The man didn't see him.
I learned later that it was mom and dad!

I was born out of love
The love of man and woman
The love of my father
The love of my mother
It's the bond I carry!

I pray that the bond will not break...

THE TASTE OF VICTORY

Nothing in this life is perfect
If everything were perfect
It would be a bore
There would be no adrenaline
Nor incentive
Nor soothing
Nothing to fight
Nothing to achieve
Everything was perfect
It takes despair
To see the relief!

It is the pursuit of perfection
That takes us to the fight
And to the reason for living
With satisfaction.

There always has to be
A problem in life
It takes commitment
Determination and will
To resolve the setback
Don't give up, it's the way
That will give us
The taste of victory and success
The taste of duty done!

A delicious sensation
Invades our entire body and spirit

It is the warrior's deserved rest!

WHAT GOD TAUGHT US

To be happy
Happy...
What a so little word
But that ends
Infinite awesomeness
Everybody
Runs after it
And so many times
We didn't even realize
That we don't have to run
Run for what?
To be happy...
It is within us
The more we run
Farther away!

Just take care
What God has taught us
Do you remember
What did God teach us?
He taught us to love
Do you know what it is to love?
Loving is extraordinarily difficult
But so rewarding and healthy!
To love is to be understanding
Tolerant and friend
To love is to give

The best we have
It's forgiving
When things get out of hand
If they hurt us
Offend and attack
It's time to use forgiveness
The good need not be forgiven
The good just needs to be cultivated
I know forgiveness
It's hard to handle
But if we strive
We will gain the necessary dexterity.

To forgive...
It is to be a great and sublime soul
Forgiveness and love
They are two friends
Who walk arm in arm
Who love, forgive
Who forgive love
It was so beautiful
See them toast to the new year!

Let's do it
We will certainly be
Very happy!

INNER LIGHT

Courage
And determination
Are essential to start
Any journey.

As we walk
Fear
Will dissipate
And trust
Will take place.

An inner light
Tiny at the beginning
Becomes bigger and bigger
Lighting up
Our steps
Like a powerful beacon
To destination
We set out to...

The achievement
Our goals!

MY MOVIE IS OVER

I wanna die.

Thus, without further ado?

No, it's not like that
It was years and years of suffering
I wanna die
Categorically
I will give myself to euthanasia
It's no use to be circumspect
I hate half words
I'm tired, very tired
To love and not be loved!

Is it any good to continue living?
Do not
I'd rather die
To have as lenitive, the same end
Suffering, suffering, suffering...
Suffering is no balm for anyone!

What kind of bullshit did I do?

Do I have leprosy?
Or some couplet pasted on my forehead?
Desired prey of any rogue?

It's decided
And decidedly
Enough for me
I got tired of false promises
You are the great love of my life
Without you, I can not live
You're the woman I've always wanted to have
I love you so much, my dear
Blah blah blah blah blah blah ...
And ending always
It's you I want to marry
They are promises of a bad payer
Go away, go to preach far away
And leave me alone with my pain!

I'm tired of mellifluous words of sour honey
Fairy tales already frighten me

I prefer to stick myself
In the roses of my garden
Than to believe in the soft talk of a rogue
Divine Father, You, who are Almighty
Protect me from people like this
Dumb people like a door
You know I'm not bad
But do not let me be a believer
Anyway, it doesn't matter now
My movie is over!

No it is not over

Who has never been crazy?
At the last moment, a flash
I'm very attached to life
Living is my desire.

Life is so brief...

I'm going to start a new movie
A funny and cheerful movie!

TIME TO SAY GOODBYE

At a time marked by time
The sun was still sleeping, it was dawn.

There was a cold, strange buzz
The sounds of the zither were barely audible
Answer my love, I don't see you
Oh this affliction tightens my chest.

I will give you heaven if you stay here with me
The goodbye time is very bitter.

After I met you
You filled my world with pampering
Cute smiles, cotton candy kisses
Passion stuffed with marshmallow
And my walk took the real meaning
I will give you heaven if you stay here with me
Immersed in the sea of love, located in my soul
I will give you warmth, healing and satiety
Relieving pain, which still torments you!

MY DREAM FELL APART

Outside it rains
The wind whistles
Snuggled under the duvet
I stare at the window
Hanging a few drops of rain
They strive not to fall.

I see your face in one of them
And I daydream
A beautiful dream
With decorated carriages
Princes, princesses and fairies
A dazzle!

I'm sad and desperate
Because meanwhile
This raindrop
Starts slipping
And it falls apart on the sidewalk ...

My dream fell apart
Just like Mofina Mendes's dream.

Epilogue:

Mofina Mendes is a false shepherd of Gil Vicente's Auto. Auto is a theatrical composition that appeared in Portugal in the Medieval Era. Gil Vicente was a playwright and poet, lived in the 15th century and was considered the father of dramaturgy in Portugal.

MY UMBRELLA

In the next house
Lives a violent neighbour
Envious and bad
Called Wind
He usually
Presses his nose to the window
Gathering food for gossip
On what goes on
In the neighbourhood.

Yesterday when I left home
There he was!
I could feel him
As I opened my brolly
He had already snuck
Behind me on tippy toes
He blew so hard
That almost floored me down
The umbrella, poor thing
Couldn't take it
The damage was not a train smash
It cost me just a pound
In Poundland shop
No need to argue...
Yet
I started yelling
I was only shutting up

When I became aphonic.

There are people
That's like the wind
They blow hate and spite
In every corner of our life
As if our life, it's a wind rose
Coming the wind from all quarters!
There are people like that
So it is today, as it was before.

I have a short fuse
When I see slutty
But I also cool down quickly
I have no anger, no grudge
I am high spirited by nature
And I only know
How to live with love
Maybe because of this...
I am a lucky woman
When I arrived at home
I noticed that my umbrella
Wasn't broken
The webbing supports
Had come unstitched
An easy fix.

The wickedness wasn't worth it
It wasn't worth it to be aphonic
But it's always like this...
It's hard not to react

When we are affronted
Anyway, evil doesn't pay!
Let there be joy!
Come on stop the stupidity
And live according to wisdom!

THE PINK BEACH

I rejoice in contentment
Behold, the longed-for day has arrived
Finally
I will make my life's dream come true
I cherished this desire
For so long and so long
Yet
Hope has always accompanied me
It was the fuel
That always fueled my dream
And didn't let it die
Hope is the faithful friend
Always present
Especially
In the hardest and saddest hours
It is like a symphony
Gifting the dark and silent night
With a beautiful melody
And the night is more catching
With the silver light
That oozes from the moon.

Oh, how much excitement
Finally
I could step on the pink sand
From the paradisiac beach
On the other side of the world!

Indonesia, Labuan Bajo, Pink Beach ...

 I slowly spell out each syllable
To be able to taste
All flavours and aromas
That the words suggest
To my brain and to my heart
In a dream dance
Danced in the warm pinky sand
In a mesmerizing scenario
To the sound
Of Beethoven's fifth symphony!

I swirl, I spread my arms
And I exult of happiness
With my heart full of heat
I rise in the air
Lighter than a feather
Letting me guide
Gently lulled
For my great and sweet love!

NOTHING LASTS FOREVER

Nothing lasts forever
Life is about change.

With every change...

A new opportunity to be reborn
A new opportunity to grow
A new opportunity for conquest!

Life is a gift ...
Of love, affection, faith and hope
There are bitter hours, hard to swallow
But there are also sweet hours
That leave us in the heart
A huge desire to love
And those are the ones to focus on!

May the night descend upon us
Loaded with blessings
And the day dawns
Tender and poetic
Shining peace!

BIOGRAPHY

MARIA DULCE LEITAO REIS

I was born in Portugal. I have two children. I once worked in Accounting and was Businesswoman at Restoration and Fashion. In 1974 I recorded two documentaries for the cinema.
Since 2006, I am living in England.

I am co-author of 56 Anthologies of Poetry and short Stories including 7 solo books in Portuguese which were translated into the English language.

Reading, writing, sudoku, photography and gardening are some of the things I love the most.
I'm also a lover of nature. I fight injustice, inequality, discrimination and violence in every way. I believe in love and peace as vehicles to make the world more balanced, more attractive, where everyone will live joyous and happy.

Poetry is an amazing and wonderful force. It is in this force that I seek the breath to move on. It gives me joy and serenity to live life with sweetness. Poetry is soul, it prolongs me in the dream and draws me closer to God.

Poetry is the air I breathe. It is the sap that circulates in my veins and brings fire and passion to every corner of my being.
Poetry is love. Poetry is life. Poetry is my bread and my stick.

BIBLIOGRAPHY

Anthologies (56)

Solar de Poetas I - Modocromia
Solar de Poetas II - Modocromia
Poesia sem Gavetas III - Pastelaria Studios
Editora
N.P.E. V
N.P.E. VI
Palavras de Cristal II - Modocromia
Palavras de Cristal III - Modocromia
Palavras de Cristal IV - Modocromia
Palavras de Cristal V - Modocromia
Alquimia dos Poetas - Incógnita Projectos
Editoriais
Mar-À-Tona/Heróis do Mar - Modocromia
Sentir D'Um Poeta - N.P.E.
Amantes da Poesia I - Editora UniVersus
Eternamente Poeta - N.P.E.
Conto de Poetas - N.P.E.
Liberdade é Poesia - N.P.E.
O Silêncio da Solidão - N.P.E.
Somos Poetas Somos Liberdade - N.P.E.
Poematis - incógnita Projectos Editoriais
Amor Eterno - N.P.E.
O sonho em Poesia vol I - Edições Hórus
Prosa Agridoce - Edições Hórus
Memórias Esquecidas no Tempo - Edições
Hórus

Um Litro de Lágrimas - Pastelaria Studios
Editora
Seis Ruas de Inspiração - Chiado Editora
Poetas d'Hoje III - Grupo de Poesia da Beira
Ria-Aveiro
Devaneios - Edições Hórus
Poemário 2017 - Pastelaria Studios Editora
Histórias para Dormir e Sonhar - Edições
Hórus
Sopro de Poesia - Pastelaria Studios Editora
Perdidamente II - Grupo Múltiplas Histórias
Perdidamente III - Grupo Múltiplas Histórias
Amantes da Poesia II - Modocromia
Amantes da Poesia III - Modocromia
Summer Rain-Heartackes Scribbled In Pain -
Bookemon/Amazon
I am a Woman - Bookemon/Amazon
Spring-window to Peace - Bookemon/Amazon
Flame-Sensual Poetry - Bookemon/Amazon
Burning Desire-Sensual Poetry -
Bookemon/Amazon
New Generation Poets - Bookemon/Amazon
World Poetry on Let There Be Peace - Amazon
The Colors Of Autumn - Bookemon/Amazon
Gogyohka Autumn Journal 2018 - Bookemon
Stairway to Heaven-
Bookemon/Amazon/Lulu
Sending Love to Mom -
Bookemon/Amazon/Lulu
Reminiscing Summer- Bookemon/ Amazon /
Lulu

The Pillar - Bookemon/ Amazon/Lulu
A Bowl of Peace - Bookemon/Amazon/Lulu
Quills in a Brighter Horizon -
Bookemon/Amazon/Lulu
Legacy - Bookemon/Amazon/Lulu
Christmas in our Hearts -
Bookemon/Amazon/Lulu
The Art of growing up -
Bookemon/Amazon/Lulu
The way we were -Bookemon/Amazon/Lulu
Poesis; Loves's poetry in 10 words
Poesis Journal March-April Book – Bookemon
The book of Hope (NHS project)

LIVROS A SOLO

Sunrise - Bookemon/Amazon/Lulu
Nascer do Sol - Bookemon/Amazon/Lulu
Emotions - Joys and Sorrows -
Bookemon/Amazon/Lulu
Emoções - Alegrias e Dores -
Bookemon/Amazon/Lulu
Tons da Vida - Bookemon/Amazon/Lulu
Shades of Life - Bookmon/Amazon/Lulu
Pearls of Dew - Bookemon/Amazon/Lulu
Pérolas de Orvalho -
Bookemon/Amazon/Lulu
Tree of Love and Serenity -
Bookemon/Amazon/Lulu
Árvore do amor e Serenidade -
Bookemon/Amazon/Lulu

Melody of Words - Bookemon/Amazon/Lulu
Melodia das Palavras -
Bookemon/Amazon/Lulu
Who are you Butterfly? -
Bookemon/Amazon/Lulu
Quem és tu Borboleta? -
Bookemon/Amazon/Lulu

Published Poetry Planet Publishing House
Cover designed by Tess Ritumalta courtesy of Pixabay
Edited by Junfil Olarte